WhatsApp Kavithaigal

Random Reflections

Muthukrishnan Chinnasamy

BookLeaf Publishing
India | USA | UK

Made with ❤ on the BookLeaf Publishing Platform
www.bookleafpub.in
www.bookleafpub.com

Dedication

Gopal Teacher, who taught us, the entire village kids everything in the Government Elementary School. English, Tamil, Science, Maths, Social Science, Politics, Sports and even Social Behaviour. An exceptionally gifted teacher, he handled all subjects for all classes from Class 1st till 5th. Often we are the labourers to carry school benches and chairs to all village functions, whether it is school related, local family related (joyful marriages, sad condolence gatherings).

He taught us how learning is built into everything. We played Volleyball with village adults and elders in the evening, discipline and skills were taught there, he made us to imbibe the quest for learning and values deeply. We made Science projects and went on tours, we helped in temples and village gatherings. We are the default volunteers for anything He and village Elders decided.

We simply learned and enjoyed.. To that man of great purpose, my little submission of Dedication.

Preface

Wife told, "You keep typing a lot of WhatsApp messages, so many groups, all the time on it". Bring the phone to the dining table, less conversations with daughters and myself, she also complained. The usual, spouse'y but correct observation. As current day professional life added, apart from daily logging onto computers, emails the omnipresent WhatsApp platform, work is done through chats and text and visual messages. With the growth of so many of its work and personal groups, it was necessary and it became a second nature to handle lot of human interactions through WhatsApp.

Personalities and personal spaces evolved within the WhatsApp environment through Family groups, Close Friends groups, College and School groups, Professional and Personal Friends groups and Hobby groups. Unfortunately most members resort to only forwarding others messages of what they think useful to others which they are not for sure most of the times, quite a few regularly using it for "Good Morning" wishes with a soulless image or some gyan'ny stuff.

Fortunately, a few deep thinking friends like me put

some own-creative comments, suggestions, some even attempted to make rules like "No daily greetings, No forwards" etc, but in a democratic world rules are the first casualty. Amongst these common daily noise, I thought we should pursue some creative tasks of our own to break that monotonous nature and also to keep the groups alive, else WhatsApp society would not forgive us, survival is the purpose of any or all human endeavours.

I started writing small, short poems, prose texts on any subject which may be of interest, relevant to daily events of public interest, even controversial to stir thoughts in fellow group members. Often in Tamil or English, translated from one to another at times as groups had members who cannot read Tamil, and some who would read only if it is in Tamil and interesting. A language skill is considered a deeper, respected pedagogic credential which it is so.

I heard/learned about this idea of Publishing from "Book Leaf", I felt excited as it resonated with my idea of establishing creative behaviour in every one of us. IEvery human story of life should be documented as humans had long invented and mastered the means to capture and store them for next generation to access and do whatever they want to do with it. Joined the platform and learned the basics through the platform ideas, sample Video Tutorial and was so impressed to know about its functions and features.

This book is a simple collections of my random reflections of life, in a poetic form. My 62+ years of learnings, observations and inferences often reflected on and from the society around me. The narrative has reality shades as they are derived from real life events and experiences. Science and reasons are subtly emphasised, at the same time tradition and cultural aspects are analysed for their merits, true or otherwise.

Enjoy the 'WhatsApp Kavithaigal"

Author - Muthukrishnan Chinnasamy, Muthu - "The Pearl"

Acknowledgements

First to my wife Gandhimathy Muthukrishnan, a life within my life. Always for me with her time, moral support and whatever is needed, Thank you Gandhi for everything.

Next to my two lovely Daughters, Mythreyi and Nethra, my remaining life. Themselves fierce critics of anything I do, me poetry writing is the Biggest Joke for them, but as I am, I decided to crack them anyway.

My college mate Kripanidhi N, who always inspired me to get into literary activities the moment we came in touch in College where we did our BE in Electronics and Communication studies together at GCT, Coimbatore, Tamilnadu, India.

Last but not least, to my Dearest friends Kumaran and Kayal Kumaran, both of them provided the needed stimulus and triggers for me to keep thinking linguistically. Especially for the so many discussions and interactions amongst four of us (including my Wife Gandhimathy) in a close WhatsApp group aptly named "Timeless". They are also the quick and fearless first critics of my musings.

1. Confusion

An agitated mind, energy in flight,
Settling, unsettling like a rainy breeze

Sparkle and shadow, intertwined,
In a quiet game that She plays
Hiding, seeking, within the same space

You flee from it, or so it seems,
Yet feel it still
Like a womb that holds you whole

In that circling hour, the mind labours
Sorting fragments, stitching meaning,
Breaking, remaking the same thought
Until silence begins to speak

So be confused
For in that sacred unrest
Begins the first hint of clarity

2. The First White Rain

The hails fell
as if the sky were in anger
Bangalore turned to Brooklyn,
streets dusted in sudden white

Each hail, layered like an onion,
peeled itself away
one by one,
melting
as the anger subsided

Sky and earth drew close,
their silence speaking.
Rain became the garland
pure, jasmine-white

and in that quiet union,
it was their honeymoon

3. Silence of the Lamb

Will you speak out
What lives in your heart ?
Will you walk up to
The edge of my patience ?

The secrets of my heart
That whisper to the wind
Are they not the music
Of your name through time ?

Will you find delight
In my loneliness ?
Will you sense and breathe
The emptiness within me ?

In star-lit eyes,
Your smile unfolds
Like the light of dawn,
The beginning of my life.

In the sun's shy glow,
Will you shine and warm ?
In the moon's cool grace,
Will you bloom in joy ?

If all my memories
Are filled by your presence,
The void in my heart
Becomes like moonlight...

When the world awakens,
Will you choose to sleep away ?
In prayer before the Divine,
Will you find your peace ?

Moments themselves
Seem to stand still
When you come near,
Even silence begins to sing

4. Small Is Big

For an ant,
a single drop of water becomes a flood
For a tiny seed,
the same drop is life
For a flower,
it is a mirror of adornment
For a butterfly,
a day's gentle bath
For a bird,
a sign that rain is near
For us,
a stirrer of thirst
A small drop
understood as a great flood

5. The Chromosomes Speak

Life in her begins
With XX chromosomes,
From which emerges
The diverging path of XY

When one X is released,
A man is formed
But she stands complete,
Bearing two X within

That first signal SRY,
A tiny gene that decides sex,
Turns the course of life
Like a whisper shaping destiny

Though we begin as one,
Fate splits into two directions

Within her, two X reside
A delicate balance of nature

Each cell chooses one to silence,
Creating a living mosaic within

From mother and father
She carries an X from each
But man, with a single X,
Carries only his mother's legacy

And so, the thread of inheritance
Flows through the mother's line
The tales of mitochondria
Echo across generations untold

Once mighty, the Y chromosome
Now shrinks along its path
From thousands of genes
To a fragile few that remain

Yet the enduring X
Sustains life's equilibrium
And thus, humanity
Continues to flourish

Between XX and XY
Lies nature's subtle harmony
An endless coded symphony
Of human existence

She (XX) is life itself
Womanhood is her name
Motherhood her calling,
And purity our (XY) aspiration and Her expectation

Look to the calico cats
Nature's mosaic revealed in quiet truth
The human race is steadied by Her,
Guarding us from oblivion

On this Women's Day, remember
In every genome we carry,
Her silent strength
Lives on

6. The Spinning World

This globe spins fast, a painted scheme,
A dizzy dance, a clever dream;
It twirls so quick, we lose our pace,
And call it life's relentless race

What if it slowed, just for a while ?
Would time then pause enough to smile ?
A week of day, a week of night
To dream in dark, to work in light

To sleep within our endless dreams,
To labor where the sunlight gleams;
To breathe between the rush and run,
And feel, at last, what life's begun

But no, this world won't ease its art,
It spins and pulls at every heart;
And somewhere far, beyond our view,
The stars just laugh at what we do

For not just space, nor time's vast sea
But galaxies, in conspiracy,
Seem set to keep us on this ride
And we just spin along inside.

The Spinning Earth, A Quiet Conspiracy

The Earth does not rush
It simply turns,
Obeying the pull of gravity
And the laws we name angular momentum

A silent spin
1670 km per hour at the equator,
Yet we feel no wind of it,
No tremor beneath our feet

Is it speed, then...
Or our stillness within it ?

Day breaks, night falls
Not because time moves,
But because we do

A rotation mistaken for urgency,
A cycle mistaken for chase

What if it slowed

Not the Earth,
But our perception of it ?

A longer dawn to understand light,
A deeper night to meet ourselves;
Where dreams are not interruptions,
But continuations

We say, “The universe conspires,”
Yet the cosmos is indifferent
No intent, no design against us;
Only motion, vast and precise

Galaxies do not hurry,
Stars do not strive
They burn, they move,
They simply are

And here we are
On a turning sphere,
Calling motion a burden,
And stillness a luxury

Perhaps the question is not
“Why does the world spin so fast ?”

But, “Why do we feel the need to keep up ?”

In a universe that only moves,
We alone create haste

And so the quiet truth remains:
Not just the universe
Not even the galaxy

But our own minds
Conspire against our peace

7. The Wife and Husband

To make a house a living soul,
She becomes its breath, she makes it whole;
A quiet flame, unseen yet true,
"I am for you, and you for me", she grew

She seeks no wealth, no claim, no part,
Yet holds a world within her heart;
A heart that none can truly own,
A love that blooms, yet stands alone

Each second beats with questions deep,
And answers that her silence keeps;
In life's long script, both joy and strife,
She writes the meaning, she is life

And he who sees with watchful eyes,
A learner beneath her silent skies;
A pen that shapes what time has planned,
An artist guided by her hand

Through her vision, he learns to be,
Through his gaze, he learns to see;
Not just a man, but one who can
Become, through love, a husband

Two halves that meet, yet stand as one,
A journey shared, never undone;
For in that bond, so deep, so true
A home is born… in me and you

மனைவி-கணவன்

ஒரு வீட்டை உயிராக்க (*மனை*)யில்
அ(*வி*)யாய்
உனக்கு நான் எனக்கு நீ என்றும் நம்பி
தனக்கு எதையும் தேடாதவள்
தேடினாலும் கிடைக்காத அவள் இதயம்
துடிக்கும் ஒவ்வொரு வினாடிகளும்
வினாக்களும் விடைகளுமாய் வாழ்வில்
பேனா எழுத்துக்கள் வடிவில்
வடிவமைக்கும் ஒரு கலைஞனாய்
படிப்பிக்க தன் (*கண்*) பார்க்கும் அ(*வன்*) -
கணவன்

8. No,No,No

Tamil is not defined by its people
Nor are its people bound by Tamil alone;
No

A language is not the measure of a race,
Nor is lineage the truth we own
No

Our pride does not live in ancient days,
Nor in echoes of a fading past;
Our rise is not in another's fall,
For such small victories never last
No

Our strength is forged in who we are,
In what we build, in how we grow;
In character, courage, and constant climb
In the will to rise, again, and so

Not in names, nor in borrowed fame,

Not in history carved in stone;
But in every step that moves us forward,
In a future we make our own

Call us what you will, define us how
We are more than words can say;
For neither Tamil nor Tamilians
Will ever fade, or drift away

We rise, we float, we surge once more,
Through every tide, through every roar;
For in our spirit, fierce and free
Lives an endless, boundless sea

We will not sink
We will rise
We will rise again

9. A Friend called Kipper

We did not know him as well as Kumarans
But It knew us as much as Them, owners
It accepted us
It liked us
It showed as much affection
It wanted us
It watched us
It listened
It stared at us with his shining eyes
It's muffled quiet footsteps making us turn
It roamed like a lonely Lion King
It was restless
Then the eternal rest came
It left a void in all of us
It went ahead to explore
Too early and extempore
Kipper, u are there
In our memories forever
Your occasional happy barks echoing as ever

10. Alone

We are born with a mother's embrace,
We live among many, in shared space;
Through laughter, bonds, and fleeting ties,
With countless souls our journey lies.

Yet in the end—when all is done,
We walk that final path, alone;
(Except where fate, abrupt and wild,
Breaks the order, undefined.)

The lone palm stands against the sky,
Teaching truths that words deny;
In silent wisdom, still and high,
It speaks of how we live and why.

A voiceless knowing, calm and deep,
That neither shouts, nor tries to keep;
It sheds its leaves, its wings, its pride,
To show what strength is found inside.

A colorless green, a nameless grace,
Rooted firm in time and space;
It does not cling, it does not plea
It simply stands in being free.

So let us not, in noise and need,
Forget this quiet, living creed;
For all we gain, for all we see
Life, at its core, is walked Alone.

11. The Decimal Poem

Let the Journey Continue...

One mountain's peak,
the foothill of the next

Two hearts unite,
life begins

Becoming **three**,
joy knows no bounds

Traveling the **four** directions,
gathering wealth and means

Nurturing the **five** landscapes,
a noble, tireless effort

With the **six**-faced one, (Lord Muruga)
devotion earns grace

Crossing the **seven** seas,
reaching higher ground

Leaving behind the **eight** dual colours,
tears and turmoil fade away

Living till **nine**ties,
desires and dreams intertwined

With (a) **ten** friends beside us,
let our life's journey continue...

12. Father - Who is also Mother (Thayumanavar)

Father – The One Who Became a Mother

"Appa"... "Ayya"... "Aiyan"
Names that time may gently bend;
Yet through all words, one truth remains
A silent strength that does not end

In our growing years, he stood,
Not in rest, but thought and deed;
Always working, always bearing
Every want, and every need

For sisters' weddings, debts he bore,
With trembling steps, yet steady will;
Through broken paths and restless nights,
He climbed, though life stood testing still

Not for himself did he endure,
But for the lives that walked ahead;

In quiet pride, he watched us rise,
With dreams he built, though words unsaid

In our success, his joy would shine,
A light that needed no display;
A heart that swelled in silent grace,
And gave itself, day after day

For in his care, so vast, so deep,
There lived a love both fierce and mild
Not just a father, firm and wise,
But one who mothered every child

And so we know, in truth profound,
Beyond all names that we can say
A father's love, when lived so full,
Becomes a mother's gentle way

13. The Beloved Ever

Forever Wife, Forever Beloved

What the heart dreams, the eyes reveal,
What you wish, I strive to fulfill;
What we dream becomes our way,
The path we choose, the lives we lay

What the world may think or say,
We shape as vows along our way;
What the Divine has softly planned,
We hold as truth, we understand

Like a shadow that walks beside,
Never distant, never denied;
In every step, in every mile,
You are my strength, my quiet smile

Not just a wife, but love's own flame,
A constant heart, forever the same;
Through changing days and passing years,

You stand beyond all doubts and fears

In you I find both home and grace,
A timeless warmth I can embrace;
A love that grows, yet stays so true,
A life made whole, because of you

With all my love, with blessings deep,
For bonds that wake and never sleep;
To the one who walks with me always
My beloved, in all my days

14. Ilakkiya and Harish

Ilakkiya, your path is bright, target (Ilakku) is right
A dream of love, a guiding light;
With grace that glows, both soft and true,
A world of beauty lives in you

Like Vishnu's calm and Shiva's fire,
A sacred bond, a shared desire;
In **Harish** stands a heart so rare,
Where love and virtue blend with care

He who once, with open soul,
Embraced the world and made it whole,
Now holds your hand, both firm and kind,
And leaves his solitary path behind

For in your touch, a truth he found,
A deeper joy, a sweeter sound;
His road no longer his alone,
But one where both your hearts have grown

“Hearts that never drift apart,”
He played Ed Sheeran's from the heart;
And if life’s song is love’s own art,
May yours be music from the start

Let laughter rise like morning sun,
Let trials fade when day is done;
In every storm, in skies of blue,
May strength and peace abide in you

Hand in hand, through time you’ll glide,
With faith and warmth your constant guide;
Two souls, once separate, now aligned,
In rhythm deep, in spirit twined

Young in years, yet wise in grace,
A timeless glow in your embrace;
For love like yours, both pure and strong,
Has known its truth all along

May every dawn bring dreams anew,
And every dusk your joys renew;
May home be where your hearts reside,
With hope forever at your side

So walk together, come what may,
Through night’s soft hush and golden day;

For love, when held both deep and true,
Will light the path ahead for you

With blessings warm, with hearts so full,
For days made bright and beautiful;
A life of song, of love's sweet art
Two hands as one, one beating heart

15. Life, A Family, Questions

Life, A Family, Questions

A family is not a throne to claim,
Nor power dressed in duty's name;
It is a vow, a quiet art
An offering made from a loving heart

Not to command, but to become,
A place where many souls are one;
Where giving shapes what we can be,
And love completes our destiny

Life itself is a patient quest
To calm the mind, to shape the rest;
To guide our words, to order our deeds,
Through time that tests, through silent needs

And when another walks in tune,
A kindred soul beneath the moon,
The journey deepens, rich and wide

Two hearts made one, walking side by side

We say we enter life with care,
A mother's touch, a presence there;
And leave this world, as fate has shown,
In solitude, each soul alone

Yet even that now stands untrue
For lives are lost, not one, but few;
Two hundred seventy hearts undone,
All gone together, save for one.

A witness left, to speak, to bear
The weight of loss too vast to share;
And in that silence, raw and deep,
We question truths we once could keep

How can the heavens still remain,
So distant from our human pain ?
How can a world so vast, so broad,
Still make us doubt the grace of God ?

And yet, perhaps, in grief we see
Not cruelty, but fragility;
A life so brief, so undefined,
A truth too heavy for the mind

So hold each bond, each fleeting breath,
For love alone outlives all death;
In fragile time, in borrowed days,
We are but sparks in passing ways

16. Life Partner

Life Partner

A youthful desire gently turned into love,
Two hearts unwaveringly merged as one

On endless journeys, joy painted vivid scenes,
With friends and family as transient travellers

Dancing, singing, laughter, and games,
With quarrels and reconciliations blending as one

He (or she) stands firm, by my side every single day
My true companion.

17. If Nature wrote a Love Story

If Nature Wrote a Love Story

If Nature were to write a tale,
Of love so soft, so pure, so pale
The rain would be the lover true,
And trees his love in shades of green and blue

He comes in whispers, slow and light,
In silver drops of tender might;
Each falling bead, a gentle kiss,
A quiet song of fleeting bliss

Upon the tips of leaves he stays,
In silent touch, in hidden ways;
She feels his presence, calm and deep,
A secret vow the earth will keep

Her emerald heart begins to glow,
In every drop that he lets flow;

She drinks his care, his soft embrace,
And blooms in quiet, shining grace

No words are said, no voices rise,
Yet truth is seen in lowered eyes;
In stillness vast, their spirits blend
Where love begins, and has no end

For in that pause, so pure, so whole,
Two beings meet in silent soul;
And there, within that sacred art
Love is born, without a heart

18. What is in a Name

Prasanth, The Quiet Strength

Even when storms begin to rise,
There's no unrest within his eyes;
A silence deep, untouched, unshaken
Where every fear is gently taken

Where chaos melts and worries fade,
A calm within is softly laid;
A space where restless thoughts depart
That stillness lives in **Prasanth**'s heart

In a world that overflows with sound,
He chooses peace that can't be found;
While others race with hurried breath,
He stands, untroubled, still as death

When voices clash and noise runs high,
He does not shout, nor question why;
In quiet ways, he understands

What slips away from louder hands

When speed is praised as victory's sign,
And haste is hailed as something fine,
He proves with grace, so firm, so true
That calm itself has power too

On paths where confusion clouds the sight,
His mind walks steady, clear, and right;
No tangled turns can lead him astray,
For peace within will light his way

And so it is, both soft and strong,
A name that feels where it belongs;
Not just a word, but truth made art
Prasanth, the stillness of a heart ✧

19. Questions

Questions

Is it rain, or is it cloud ?
A tender hush, or thunder loud ?
Is it a burden, or a scar ?
A wound within, or who we are ?

Is it love, or passing grace ?
A fleeting touch, a warm embrace ?
Is it a dream, or waking sight ?
A shadow lost within the light ?

Is it the eye, or what it sees ?
A restless storm, or quiet seas ?
Is it a story left untold ?
Or truth that trembles, shy yet bold ?

Is it a path, or wandering feet ?
A broken rhythm, incomplete ?
Is it a word, or silent plea ?

A fading echo, or destiny ?

In life we ask, again, again
Yet answers drift like falling rain;
For in each doubt, and every call,
Perhaps, there is no **"is"** at all

20. My Fair Ladies

My Fair Ladies, A Life Written in Love

Perhaps when we are sent into this world,
God writes a quiet contract
Not of fate alone, but of love
Binding us, gently,
To the women who will shape our journey

Mine unfolds not in chance,
But in grace, one by one.

Ammamma

A woman of quiet strength and fierce independence.
In her home, I did not just grow, I was formed.
Through fields she walked, through life she carried alone,
Yet never alone in spirit
She taught us contentment without compromise,
Activity without complaint,
And dignity without demand
Even in her final days, she stood tall

As if life itself had learned resilience from her

Amma

A mother who brought life into this world
Almost by herself,
And then spent a lifetime building others
Her hands knew no rest
Between home and soil,
Between duty and love
From her, we learned not just to work,
But to respect work
And to expect strength, not comfort,
From life and from ourselves

Akka #1 - Kanakamani

The first light of affection I ever knew
In her love, there were no conditions,
No hesitations, only giving
A heart pure, obedient, unwavering
A quiet promise that love can remain simple

Akka #2 - Mythili

Gentle in body, yet vast in spirit
She carried more than her share,
Yet never let it show
In her presence, fairness felt natural,
Grace felt effortless

Even now, in her absence,
She teaches
That love does not end, it echoes

Akka #3 - Tamilarasi

Not just a sister, but a mirror of my being
We grew together
In play, in struggle, in decisions too early for our years
Courage was not taught; it was lived between us
Even today, we walk as reflections
Two thoughts, one understanding

My Wife, My Life - Gandhimathy

Some meetings are not coincidences;
They are recognitions
The moment I saw her, I knew
And life simply followed that knowing
Thirty-three years later,
Through storms and stillness,
Our love has not aged
It has deepened
She is not part of my life
She is its meaning
God's contract fulfilled in perfection

My Kido #1 - Mythreyi

The day she was born,

Joy found a permanent home in my heart
And every day since,
She reminds me
That happiness can grow

My Kido #2 - Nethra
As if life believed in symmetry,
She came to complete the circle
With her, laughter doubled,
And love found new depth
In her, I see echoes of Ammamma
Strength reborn, softly

And so I stand
Not as one man alone,
But as a life shaped, guided, and held
By these extraordinary women

On this Women's Day,
My gratitude is not in words alone
But in the life I have lived because of them

To them
And to all the women who quietly shape our worlds

With love, with reverence, always

21. The Pearl

The Pearl

In shifting tides of time's domain,
Do we dissolve or shall remain ?
Do we endure like steadfast stone,
Or fade where silent winds have blown ?

The question lives in "who are we ?"
A fleeting doubt, or clarity;
For in a simple "yes" or "no,"
The path we take begins to show

With every choice, the mind made clear,
The fog will fade, the way appear;
And from the depths where doubts once swirled,
A truth emerges—like a **Pearl**

22. Social Distance

Social Distance

The worker became a "labour class,"
The owner rose as "industrial mass";
Titles changed, yet truths remain
Old divides in a modern frame

The one below, the one above,
Defined not by worth, but words we love;
Language itself draws lines so clear,
A subtle gap we fail to hear

Even English laughs in tone
"Happy Labour Day", a paradox shown;
A greeting bright, yet laced with strain,
Where toil and cheer don't quite align

Between these names, a distance stays,
Widened softly through our ways;
A space that speaks, though none may say,

Of unequal paths we walk each day

May this divide begin to bend,
May edges soften, gaps transcend;
Till ground once split becomes a plain,
Where all may stand, and none feel pain

And so this wish, both light and true,
From one who sees the shifting view
A working man, with a smiling plea,
And his "boss-wife's" kind decree

23. Son of the Earth

Son of the Earth

Born in the cradle of Earth, you rise
O Sun, beneath her endless skies;
You warm her breast with golden flame,
And gift all life in light's own name

A mother's child, yet vast and bright,
You wake the world with tender light;
From dawn's first breath to twilight's end,
On you all living beings depend

That light became the farmer's seed,
A silent force for every need;
They tilled the soil, the Earth's own frame,
And mixed their sweat with hope and flame

Their labor flowed like living streams,
Their hands were filled with fragile dreams;
They sowed their faith in furrows deep,

While seasons watched and skies would keep

The soil turned mother, rich and kind,
The seed a child, with life aligned;
Beneath your gaze, so warm, so wise,
The crops like rising worlds would rise

And when the grain in fullness stood,
A gift of toil, of sun, of good
They placed it first before your sight,
And said, "This is your fruit, O Light."

From sunrise gold to sunset's glow,
Where fields of silent prayers still grow;
Pongal is not a day alone,
But gratitude in seeds once sown

A prayer that lives through every hour,
In farmer's hand, in sunlight's power;
A bond of Earth, of toil, of grace
A sacred rhythm time can't erase

O Sun, though Earth may call you son,
And all begins where you have begun
It is the farmer, strong and wise,
Who turns your light to life that thrives

For in his hands, the hunger of man
Becomes the grain, becomes the plan;
A father's role, both firm and true
To shape the world we journey through

So here we bow, with hearts aware,
To light, to soil, to toil, to care;
For in this union, deep and grand,
Lives the truth of life and land

24. Sunday

Let Us Praise the Sunday

Among the days, she blooms like spring,
In passing hours, soft peace she brings;
In simple clothes, a carefree delight,
In waiting hearts, a spark so bright

In meals she adds a richer taste,
In feelings, warmth that none can waste;
Each moment when our eyes close slow,
Her presence turns to dreams aglow

She frees the mind from silent strain,
From weekday rush and hidden pain;
With family near and friendships true,
She grants the time we seldom knew

For duties done with lighter will,
For bonds that time alone can fill;
A day for rest, for love, for grace,

That gently life itself embraces

A quiet gift, a soulful stay,
That fills our breath in its own way;
O day of warmth, of joy's own art
You heal the mind, you hold the heart

So let us pause, and gratefully say,
In praise of this life-giving day
A blessing wrapped in golden ray:
All glory to Sunday

25. Tamil Palindrome, A puzzle

Will clouds ever scatter ?
Will flowers choose to fade ?
Do cattle really run,
Can an elephant turn into a cat ?

A child asks, learning the world,
As a magical chariot rolls in
Do the drums forget their rhythm ?
Can a garland droop like evening light ?

மேகமே கலைக
பூ வாடவா
மாடுஓடுமா
யானை பூனையா
பாப்பா வினவி கற்க
மாயமா தேருவருதே
மேளதாளமே தாளாதா
துவளுவது மாலா போலாமா
-தந்த விகடகவி

26. The Cost of Living

The Cost of Living

This world is not unjust, nor blind
It is, by design, a market of the mind;
For every height that we attain,
The price ascends, again, again
For comfort, honor, fleeting peace,
The cost will rise, will never cease

What we gather asks to be kept,
What we achieve must be adept;
Maintained, renewed, refined with care
For nothing gained stays always fair.
Even joy we claim as ours
Begins to fade, like fragile flowers

But loss alone is stark and true,
It makes no deals, it bargains through;
It knows no inflation, no shifting scale,
It comes, it takes without a tale.

Yet leaves behind, in silent grace,
A clearer sight, a steadier pace

We lose our youth and learn of time,
We lose our strength and measure climb;
We lose our people and then we see
The weight they held, invisibly

In a life where all is priced and sold,
Where worth is weighed in bought and told,
There lies one truth beyond all trade
A loss no currency can persuade

It shrinks our days to fleeting breath,
Uninsured moments, untouched by death;
Irreplaceable, raw, and real
A quiet truth we cannot conceal

Perhaps true joy was never found
In things that stay, in things that bound;
But in what came, and passed us by
A whispered laugh, a fading sigh

In a world that longs to cost us more,
To raise its price forevermore,
The greatest thrift we may compose
Is making peace with what we lose

Marina. O Marina

O Marina, My Marina

O Marina, O Marina,
Yet beside me no Kareena;
Still my heart begins to ride,
Like a galloping tide by the shore so wide

On the sands, where dreams take flight,
Toy-horse spins in rings of light;
A childlike joy in circling gleam,
A fleeting ride, a painted dream

Along the world's long stretching shore,
Where waves return forevermore;
The metro hums in distant speed,
A pulse that matches every need

By night, the stars in lamps appear,
Soft glowing lights both far and near;
Like constellations brought to land,

Held gently in a human hand

Fireworks burst, then fade in rain,
A fleeting joy, a shining stain;
Yet even as the colours fall,
The night still holds them, one and all

Nature laughs, and people play,
In woven rhythms of the day;
A dance where earth and hearts unite,
In simple wonder, shared delight

And somewhere beyond what eyes can see,
The gods look on in harmony;
Approving smiles in silent grace,
As joy unfolds in time and space

The festival may come to end,
But love remains, no bounds to bend;
For in that shore, in that embrace,
Lives something vast no time can erase

28. The Two, The One

The Two

Our journey of life is vast,
The path is long,
With trials to cross,
With language as our companion
Children become
The fellow travellers of our path.
Parents serve
As our guiding lights.
Friends are
Mirrors to our soul
Together just the two of us
We pause, we rest,
Sing slowly,
Dance gently,
And in the quiet weariness of it all,
Exits first, leaving

The One

29. The Water

Who Are You ?

The cloud that veils the silver moon,
Then melts to rain, a gentle boon;
The thirst it soothes, the life it gives,
In every drop, the whole world lives

Like rivers dreaming of the sea,
In restless flow, forever free;
Like time that sows the forest's birth,
A silent promise to the earth

A mother's arms that hold the hills,
A teacher in the breeze that thrills;
A song that hums through leaves so light,
A whispering voice in day and night

A god that guards all living breath,
A force that balances life and death;
A father's hand that shapes our way,

Through night's dark veil to break of day

In every form, unseen yet true,
The world exists because of you;
Without your grace, none could endure
O tell me, who are you ?

I am Water

www.ingramcontent.com/pod-product-compliance
Lightning Source LLC
Chambersburg PA
CBHW070646240926
51846CB00003BA/797
* 9 7 8 9 3 7 5 4 3 0 0 4 9 *